On The Front Line with
ROYAL WARRIORS

ILONA PARUNAKOVA
REGELINE SABBAT

Copyright © 2021 by Ilona Parunakova & Regeline Sabbat

On The Front Line with ROYAL WARRIORS

All rights reserved. No part of this publication may be reproduced, distributed, or transmitted in any form or by any means, including photocopying, recording, or other electronic or mechanical methods, without the prior written permission of the publisher, except in the case of brief quotations embodied in critical reviews and certain other noncommercial uses permitted by copyright law. For permission requests, write to the publisher, addressed "Attention: Permissions Coordinator," at info@beyondpublishing.net

Quantity sales special discounts are available on quantity purchases by corporations, associations, and others. For details, contact the publisher at the address above.

Orders by U.S. and Canada trade bookstores and wholesalers. Email info@BeyondPublishing.net

The Beyond Publishing Speakers Bureau can bring authors to your live event. For more information or to book an event contact the Beyond Publishing Speakers Bureau speak@BeyondPublishing.net

The Author can be reached directly at BeyondPublishing.net

Manufactured and printed in the United States of America distributed globally by BeyondPublishing.net

New York | Los Angeles | London | Sydney

ISBN Hardcover: 978-1-63792-184-5

Table of Contents

CHAPTER ONE: LEADERSHIP WITH SERVANT HEARD	7
Mind Quality as a Servant Leader	9
Integrity	9
Humility	9
Flexibility	11
Resilience	11
CHAPTER TWO: STEWARDSHIP	13
Empathy	14
CHAPTER THREE: SERVANT LEADERS IDENTITY	16
CHAPTER FOUR: ROYAL WARRIOR	19
Why It's Important	26
CHAPTER FIVE: REMOVING DOUBT AND FINDING STILLNESS	21
CHAPTER SIX: OUR LEGACYS POWER	24
CHAPTER SEVEN: THE VALUE IN YOUR LIFE	31
CHAPTER EIGHT: LEARNING TO CONCENTRATE YOUR EYES	35
CHAPTER NINE: YOUR INNER EYE'S WINDOW	40
CHAPTER TEN: BE KIND TO OTHERS	43
Because God is Kind	44
Because God Forgives	46
Why Is This Important	48
My Final Thoughts	48
Power of Dreams	49
God is by My Side	50
CHAPTER ELEVEN: You Are Gid's Servants	51
Leaders Serve	51
Serve From a Full Cup, not an Empty Cup	51

It's Not About you, It's About Serving Others	52
CHAPTER TWELVE: YOU ARE NOT ALONE ON YOUR LIFE JOURNEY	54
God is with you wherever you go	54
You Have Support from Your Community	55
CHAPTER THIRTEEN: YOU CAN OVERCOME THE CHALLENGES IN YOUR LIFE	57
God First	57
Resilient Mindset	58
CHAPTER FOURTEEN: YOU ARE A LEADER WHO IS A ROYAL WARRIOR	61
Royal Warrior Defined	61
Royal Warriors Never Give Up	61
CHAPTER FIFTEEN: BE COURAGEOUS!	65
Face Your Challenges	65
CHAPTER SIXTEEN: ACHIEVE YOUR GOALS	68
"Action"	68
CHAPTER SEVENTEEN: BE EFFECTIVE IN WHAT YOU DO	71
Leadership	71
CHAPTER EIGHTTEEN: LIVE YOUR DREAMS	73
Stop Drifting in Your Life	73
CHAPTER NINETEEN: STEP ONTO THE FRONT LINES	75
Faith over Fear	75
CHAPTER TWENTY: YOU ARE ON THE FRONT LINES WITH EACH INDIVIDUAL	77
Who is God's Servant. Keep Going and Serve!	77

Chapter One

LEADERSHIP WITH SERVANT HEART

*A genuine leader is not a searcher for consensus,
but a molder of consensus.*
Martin Luther King, Jr.

Lead from the back, and let others believe they are in front.
Nelson Mandela

Leadership is as old as the hills, but the true history of the term is modern. The first known use goes back to 1821, when the word leader and the suffix "ship"—indicating rank—were joined (as in the position of a leader). The word leader has an ancient pedigree: "one who leads", "to guide, bring forth". "Leader" or "leadership" is not derived from Latin or Greek. The closest word in antiquity regarding leadership is the Latin verb *ducere*— "to guide, consider, and respect"— and, strangely, to lead and guide in the present Romanian language.

If you study the etymology of the word "leadership" and its historical cousin, *ducere*, you can start understanding why our modern comprehension of what leaders do and what leadership is, is so complex and variable. The term has many meanings: direction, guidance, transformation, facilitation, orchestration, and more; and each of those many connotations signifies types of conduct: directive, transformative, facilitative, leader as steward, servant leader, and more.

In Matthew 20:25-28 (NLT), this is what Jesus said about leadership: "But Jesus called them together and said, 'You know that the rulers in this world lord it over their people, and officials flaunt their authority over those under them. But among you, it will be different. Whoever wants to be a leader among you must be your servant, and whoever wants to be first among you must become your slave. For even the Son of Man came not to be served, but to serve others and to give his life as a ransom for many.'"

There is a lovely Christian phrase we use to name the kind of leadership Jesus speaks about in Matthew 20—a "leading servant". The aim of our leadership in Christ is not to gain power, but to serve.

Leadership does not mean our names are known. It's about making the name of God known. We must make known His name and have the ability to love and respect the people we care for by exercising our authority with the grace we have been given.

Whether you're the CEO of a group, an older sibling, a drum major of a high school band, or a church volunteer, everyone leads someone. So, how can you become a servant leader?

Mind Quality of A Servant Leader

Integrity

"To do righteousness and justice is more acceptable to the LORD than sacrifice." — Proverbs 21:3 (ESV)

As a servant leader, integrity is possibly the most critical trait. It is the basis on which all other attributes of leadership are formed. Proverbs 21:3 recalls Jesus' invitation to walk in the paths of justice and righteousness. Our actions should reflect our faith.

As true servant leaders, we cannot cheat, lie, nor manipulate our way to the top. We're called to do something completely new and countercultural – to be honest. Jesus tells us to humble ourselves and live with integrity.

Integrity is a deliberate lifestyle that reflects general honesty and excellent character. But we stumble, and we fall (since, after all, we are human). However, true servants can confess their sins before God. Living with integrity is an effective method of witnessing to those who look up to us, above all in the face of problems and temptations.

Humility

"Since God chose you to be the holy people He loves, you must clothe yourselves with tenderhearted mercy, kindness, humility, gentleness, and patience." — Colossians 3:12 (NLT)

One of the hardest things to realize is that we may not know or practice all these attributes to which we are called in Colossians 3:12.

With the Internet at the tip of our fingers, a few pages in a search engine might be appealing and convince us we are subject matter experts. It may be easy to isolate ourselves in a bubble of self-confidence, to reject any view which does not correspond with our own. The power and authority of being a leader is a powerful draw to the addict.

A servant leader is someone who has made room to learn from other leaders' experiences and practices. In the leadership of Christian servants, we should be prepared to learn from and listen to those we lead, because we know they are of great value and worth. The truth is that they might have better ideas than we have or that we might not have an objective or mature viewpoint.

Have you ever heard a story about another's culture, or gone to a place where everyone looks different from you? Have you ever tried genuine food from another country?

One of the most gratifying experiences is the opportunity to meet people from different backgrounds who may share their views and stories. Learning about someone else's path allows us to broaden our vision of the Kingdom of God—it's a wonderful place full of people from all over the world!

Flexibility

"I know how to live on almost nothing or with everything. I have learned the secret of living in every situation, whether it is with a full stomach or empty, with plenty or little. For I can do everything through Christ, who gives me strength." — Philippians 4:12-13 (NLT)

Servant leaders need flexibility–they must be prepared to adjust to their situations and environments. Life can hand you unexpected situations or problems. But instead of allowing these situations to produce wrath, bewilderment, or panic, servant leaders know that in every scenario, God is present. You are willing to practice flexibility and actively call for change!

It might be tempting to get locked into routines, to do things one way. But the ability of a servant leader to recognize change as a potential for growth and faith helps that person lead well.

Resilience

"Therefore, since we are surrounded by so great a cloud of witnesses, let us also lay aside every weight, and the sin which clings so closely, and let us run with endurance the race that is set before us, looking to Jesus, the founder and perfecter of our faith, who for the joy that was set before Him endured the cross, despising the shame, and is seated at the right hand of the throne of God." — Hebrews 12:1-2 (ESV)

The first two lines of Hebrews 12 uses the image of running to define a life of resilience. Resilience results from developing spiritual endurance to the point where, in difficult conditions, you thrive. If you've ever trained for a marathon, you know it doesn't happen in a day. You start with short distances and build to longer runs. You get blisters and need water breaks, but you can eventually go further and longer.

Life is always going to have challenges: struggles we cannot win, mountains we cannot climb, and dark depths with no apparent way out, tunnels with no light at the end. Resilience can only happen in the Christian life when we look at Jesus.

But the constant presence of God amid the hardships of life is our source of comfort. He doesn't always repair our circumstances, and sometimes, our hoped-for timeline isn't His solution, but He always helps us get through – with love, strength, patience, and more. When we depend on our strength and ourselves, we will fail every time—in our race, we will faint and drop out.

The leaders of the servants realize that problems are real and life is challenging, but God controls them. Resilience is not a lack of fear, challenges, or shortcomings. Resilience is the ability to bounce back and push through with the knowledge that God has allowed us to persist because He is our final source of strength.

Chapter Two

STEWARDSHIP

"As each has received a gift, use it to serve one another, as good stewards of God's varied grace." — 1 Peter 4:10 (ESV)

God has given His people so many distinct spiritual gifts. Can you imagine how life would be if everybody thought, looked, and acted the same? The world might be boring place to live.

Therefore, while being effective financial managers is certainly something God wants us to do, it is not the *only* thing we manage! Your mind probably goes immediately to money when you hear the phrase stewardship. One of the definitions of Merriam-Webster is "the cautious and responsible management of something that is entrusted to one's attention".

So, though being effective financial managers is something God undoubtedly wants from us, it is equally crucial to be excellent stewards of God's people in our lives.

A servant leader views individuals as worthy of God and manages their time and abilities appropriately. This kind of leader points out what is good and truthful about the people they lead, teaching them how to serve

God wisely. A servant leader, knowing he is not his own, uses his time for the glory of God. When you interact with this type of individual, you're going to know it. You will leave conversations as if you and God value them and your gifts are exploited by the Kingdom. This is a worthy example!

Empathy

"Be happy with those who are happy, and weep with those who weep."
— ***Romans 12:15 (NLT)***

When you have been injured, did a friend or family member sit with you? Have you ever received a friend's encouraging note when you needed it most? Think about what it meant to have a person show sympathy to you in your struggles.

Empathy is vital for a servant leader. It helps you comprehend what somebody feels. It is easy to focus too much on the duties and the jobs we want to accomplish. Work is crucial and the achievement of goals is vital! But, if we don't *care* about people, we can start to regard individuals as issues to be resolved, rather than people to be cherished.

A servant leader should see people through Jesus' eyes. This is the kind of leader people follow! If we take time out of our day to empathize and put ourselves in the shoes of those around us, we become more like Jesus. Whenever Jesus met someone who hurt or needed encouragement, He looked upon them and had compassion for them. *Then*, He acted.

Leadership may appear intimidating. It's a big duty. But servant leadership also brings the opportunity to bear witness to others and to show them Jesus, which is not always possible in other positions.

Take some time today to reflect on the people God invites you to lead in your life. And when the time comes to make decisions within this capacity, ask yourself that famous question: "What would Jesus do?"

Questions To Consider

- How conscious am I of a desire or lack of desire to serve others today?
- Do those who can give me nothing back benefit from my leadership (or at least not feel further deprived)?
- Are those whom I lead more likely to become leader-servants themselves?

Chapter Three

SERVANT LEADERS: IDENTITY

"A leader is one who knows the way, goes the way, and shows the way."
– John Maxwell

"Leadership is lifting a person's vision to high sights, the raising of a person's performance to a higher standard, the building of a personality beyond its normal limitations."
– Peter Drucker

The word "identity" in the English language is derived from both a French origin – identité, ydemtité, ydemptité —defined as "the quality of being the same, sameness", – and from a late Latin origin – identitās (inflectional stem identitāt-) –meaning "the quality of being the same, the condition or fact that an entity is itself and not another thing". The Bible identifies *identity* as 'the revelation about man, his nature, life, and destiny", and identity is one of the fundamental topics of the Bible, along with the Revelation about God and salvation.

I had a long and arduous search for my identity. Once I began, numerous false voices in my thoughts sought to disturb my unique journey of adventure and self-discovery. 1 Peter 5:7-8 states, "Be sober-minded; be watchful. Your adversary, the devil, prowls around like a roaring lion, seeking someone to devour." I sought and sought, and finally, I started to see the truth: I didn't need permission from anyone to be who I was. I didn't need anybody's support or permission or for anyone to accept me. This was an awesome moment! I started to think about how I could let go of the burden I'd carried for so long, of needing to please other people; of giving them my best in order to receive a reward from them. I had felt it almost impossible to translate my feelings of self-rejection into genuine, true liberation for so long. See, I think "freedom will free you," but first, there is a death of sorts. We must say goodbye to our old self and leave behind the old ways of thinking that haven't brought us to anything.

One day, I felt the chains and fetters falling off me. This was the day I left behind my anguish and found liberation. This was the moment I could honestly say, "I know! I know! I know who I am!" I can honestly say now that I don't need to hear words of encouragement, mercy, or admiration— because I know who I am, and it has nothing to do with the outside world, nor what others think of me. When, instead of the words of other people, we start to let go and achieve true peace, we put this knowledge of who we are on the foundation of our hearts — which is the heart of God. Psalms 16:8-11 informs us, "I have set the Lord always before me; because he is at my right hand, I shall not be shaken. Therefore, my heart is glad, and my whole being rejoices; my flesh also dwells secure...."

If I could post a public slogan, it would be something like this: "Do not build your identity on any one's opinion. Know who you are. *Know who you are.* You are the masterpiece of God."

Questions To Consider

- How can you renew your mind by manifesting your dreams? What happens when you speak these words out loud?

- Have you ever seen how your fear of people's opinions affects you? Your life? One thing you may do in these times is to return to your faith and reset your heart to the voice of God.

Chapter Four

ROYAL WARRIOR

"Cowards shrink from challenges, weaklings flee from them, but warriors wink at them." – **Matshona Dhliwayo**

"A warrior conquers more in one day than a coward in a lifetime." – **Matshona Dhliwayo**

The word "warrior" comes from the Old North French *guerroieor*, "a warrior, soldier, combatant, one who wages battle", and *werreier*, to "wage war". It initially emerged in the 14th century in English.

According to 1 Peter 2: 9, all servant leaders are royal warriors. A royal warrior is a person of royal blood who engaged in warfare, a soldier. In Ephesians 6:12, the Bible says, "For we are not fighting against people made of flesh and blood, but against the evil rulers and authorities of the unseen world, against those mighty powers of darkness who rule this world, and against wicked spirits in the heavenly realms" (NLT).

All that happens in the visible, physical world is closely tied to the fight that takes place in the invisible, spiritual world.

The results of the conflict in the invisible world are evident in our strained and ruined relationships, emotional instability, mental fatigue, physical fatigue, and much more. We also need spiritual vision—to realize who we are in Christ and in everything that involves us. God has equipped us with all we need to win the spiritual battles we face, but we must know, believe, and act upon them. We must recognize and use the weapons of our spiritual warfare through prayer. Ephesians 6:10-20

Why It's Important

2 Corinthians 10:4-5 says, "For the weapons of our warfare are not carnal, but mighty through God to the pulling down of strongholds. Casting down imaginations, and every high thing that exalted itself against the knowledge of God, and bringing into captivity every thought to the obedience of Christ."

The enemy uses strength, influence, and weakness to attack us often. Thus, we must carefully determine the origins of the attacks and adopt methods to protect ourselves in the might of God. Consider your areas of greatest strength and weakness. Keep an eye on these two regions, and protect yourself with prayers. We fight a spiritual war with an opponent whose main technique is deception. This enemy can only be overcome by God's spiritual resources, which are activated and empowered by prayer.

Chapter Five

REMOVING DOUBT AND FINDING STILLNESS

"Doubt your doubts before you doubt your faith."
- President Dieter F. Uchtdorf

If we are reluctant, we ask. We doubt when we ask. This doubt is poisonous to our souls. Remember that our words need not be as lovely as an iris; they could be like weeds or just a few little stones—not gems. All we need to do is pay attention to ourselves and the world around us, fix a few words, and try not to make them complex. Life is not a contest, but, rather, a doorway to thanks.

Do we often wonder whether we should embrace our words and say them loudly or worry if they are awkward and imperfect? We ought to accept silence, as much as our confidence in grace, for precious moments come to our minds in silence – and, if we are not still, it may fade like smoke over the altar. For 1 Samuel 12:16 reminds us, "Now, therefore, stand still and see this great thing that the Lord will do before your eyes." When we come from our hearts, clear intellect, and a compassionate view, we have the soft words and confidence to say "yes" to our lives as much as we are empowered to say "no." Each of them is just as significant.

I recognized how guilty I was in the most vital moments of my life when I confronted my wrongdoings. I could name every act that had robbed me of my identity God meant for me: I have stolen; I have scorned; I have perverted; I have been cruel; I was a scoffer; I slandered, deceived, lied, and ridiculed. I disobeyed, abused, and defied; I have been corrupt; I have been hostile, stubborn, and immoral. I was spoiled, and I went astray easily. 1 John 1:9 tells us, "If we confess our sins, He is faithful and just to forgive us our sins and to cleanse us from all unrighteousness." Suddenly, I've been able to switch the script and return to God after naming all the attributes I displayed in my life that left me confused. I was and am adored. I was and am worthy.

I began to learn English in the fifth grade. Quickly, I learned to understand sentences that told me who I was: I am not a cat, I am a girl. The new English terms seemed like candy in my language. I liked the word "girl" and felt more complete, since it suited who I was – it symbolized a new world.

Now, today, after I've become strong in my faith and taken the brave leap into the depths of my identity, my life sentence is more than simply, "I'm a girl." My phrase of life would be: "I have been saved. I'm God Almighty's royal daughter."

Questions To Consider

- Can you think you of a time you doubted yourself? If so, why did you doubt? What happened? How did you feel?
- God forgives us when we recognize our wrongdoing, and there is suddenly space for light to pour in. Have you forgiven yourself for what you are embarrassed by and made a place for light? If not, what must you do to purify the place inside you, so that you can hear God's voice more easily?
- Name your life's motto.

Chapter Six

OUR LEGACY'S POWER

"The greatest legacy one can pass on to one's children and grandchildren is not money or other material things accumulated in one's life, but, rather, a legacy of character and faith." – **Billy Graham**

The phrase "legacy" can imply different things for different people. Some simply don't care, because they don't want to leave a legacy. But for others, the phrase legacy evokes visions of a monument built to a great life, a fantastic career, and splendid deeds. Others define a legacy as leaving family members—especially children—with properties to make their lives pleasant and plentiful. Philanthropists think the word means to leave something to society as a whole, to help many people generally.

A legacy is defined as what is left after a person dies – money or assets. After we're gone, what people remember of us is our legacy. This is what we left behind. We don't have to be a rock star or a president to leave something. Everyone who is serious about their future should plan on leaving a legacy, and we have the luxury of deciding how the legacy is implemented. We need to spend time considering how we want to be remembered. Have we ever wondered whether we have made a positive and lasting difference? Will anything you did here last after you are gone?

My grandfather Garegin, on Sashik's side, was one of the most intelligent, brightest, and bravest people I've ever known. The way he walked, spoke, and held himself in public attracted the interest of other people and drew attention. I could use a thousand words to describe his character: he was a brave military warrior, a military soldier, a defendant, a guard, and an army guard.

During the Second World War, Garegin survived the most terrible massacre by the brutal and merciless Turkish soldiers of the Ottoman Empire. He lost both his parents, who were decapitated before his innocent eyes. When he fled to avoid death, he was not quite nine years old. One sibling was tied to his chest as the other one—only five—raced beside him, holding his hand firmly. His brother, in his rush to escape the massacre, tripped on a stone. In this split second, Garegin had to face the most life-changing and awful decision of his life: return to try and save his brother with the chance they'd all be killed or keep going and rescue himself and his youngest brother. He elected to continue to run. "Is the world going to judge me?" he asked himself. Would he ever forgive himself for letting his brother die? This decision would haunt him throughout his life.

Our choices affect our lives. Every choice becomes part of who we are. What choices did you make that affected your life or the lives of others? Have you ever looked back with regret and wished you had made another choice? If so, you're not alone. We all have regrets. But if we recall that the right road is a choice taken in faith and not from our own intellect, how can we be filled with sorrow? Proverbs 16:9 states, "The heart of man plans the way, but the Lord establishes his steps." Or as Proverbs 19:21 states, "Many are the plans in the mind of man, but it is the purpose of the Lord that will stand."

Our decisions help shape who we are. So does our surname, another vital aspect of our identity that we receive when we are born. A surname will follow us throughout our lives, unless we change it through marriage, adoption, or some other means. We change our surname for many good reasons. Family names are relatively new in various places of the world, such as Armenia. It was only in the 19th century, when the census began, that surnames formally began to be registered and proof required.

My surname was behind it — like all our surnames, including my grandfather Garegin, and how he had spent his life. As much as he was valiant and courageous, he could not grasp that anything could be seen beyond the world... a spiritual world and a life as we learn from Corinthians 4:18. "...we look not to the things that are seen, but to the unseen things. For the things that are seen are transient, but the unseen things are eternal."

Garegin only perceived the world around him; the spiritual had no part in his way of thinking and being. Before World War I, Garegin was a ruler and territorial governor. He had been royalty. However, once the Armenians embraced Christianity as the religion of their country (Armenia was the first country to accept Christianity officially), they had no place of worship. So Garegin built a church. Now, people had a dilemma: they had a church, but no one to guide them. They didn't have a priest. When this became clear, Garegin resigned his power to become his people's priest.

This choice affected Garegin's life profoundly. When he saw himself as a mighty monarch, it fit his rational thinking. But once he became a priest, he began to explore deeper and deeper into life. In doing so, he saw something he had never seen before; a new logic was unleashed within him. Along with this new rationale, he saw the fullness of judgment and inflexibility of his rule and authority. He saw, felt, and appreciated this new spiritual "logic" that began to break this judgment. Suddenly, he saw that he accepted a new way of being. The Bible teaches that God comes to us in "faces of poverty, of beggars, of hunger, of thirst, of loneliness, of abandonment, of suffering," and says: "Since it has become one of my lesser brethren, you have made me (...), because you have not done this to one of the least, you have not done it to me."

In our world, power, authority, and wealth are easy to value – exactly as my grandpa Garegin did. In the spiritual life, by contrast, a life of love, everyone is cherished, including the impoverished, the sick, lonely, and abandoned. But let's not wait until we meet the hungry or beggars or homeless. If we can help relieve the misery of anyone who comes to us, even if we don't want to, we will, because it's that person who will judge us on the last day.

Today, people suffer more than ever from loneliness, despair, and spiritual pain. If a person lives next to us who is suffering and we do nothing to aid him, he will judge us on the final day. This is the genuine meaning of governance and wealth as a Solomon.

This does not imply we should be naïve and aid anyone who begs us, without thinking. In Proverbs 14:18, we are reminded of this: "The naïve inherit foolishness, but the sensible are crowned with knowledge." After all, it is difficult to think that if we give an alcoholic money, he uses that money to buy alcohol. If we embrace a person and meet them where they are—without judgment—if we listen to them and think about what they need and how to help, this is perhaps the best type of aid we can give. It is sufficient to treat somebody else as a human being who has value. The healing has occurred. "This is my commandment, that as I loved you, you love one another" (John 15:12).

My grandpa Garegin might be of royal blood, but the purest quality of royalty is sensitivity—and this is the logic in God's kingdom that says we cannot be soulless, indifferent to someone else or his needs. Man must mean more to us than money, our joys, luxuries, or status. Jesus says in the Bible, "If you've done it to one of my younger brothers, then you've done that to me."

It can be a boy who needs the time of his dad. Or a sister who needs assistance. The child often hears from his dad, "I'm tired; tomorrow we'll play, but not now." Aid to another starts at home, as first Timothy 5:8 shows: "But if anyone does not provide for his relatives, and especially for members of his household, he has denied the faith and is worse than an unbeliever." I feel humbled when I reflect on my legacy and the formula of success my grandfather lived. I am proud to carry his heritage forward to help others, as I follow the guidelines of 1 Peter 4:10, "Each of you should use whatever gift you have received to serve others, as faithful stewards of God's grace in its various forms." Now that I've got it, I'm moved in my core. I have come to know that I have a responsibility to carry the message and mission of my grandfather forward and deliver it to people who most need it. That's my responsibility and my fate. What is your legacy, and how does it affect your life and the lives of others? We are all worthwhile and must carry on with the work to which we have been called. This is our personal and spiritual responsibility.

Our legacy is a big part of our identity, and understanding ourselves is the best discovery we can make in our life on earth. When I wrote this book, I went on my journey of self-discovery, dove deeper into my ancestry, and unearthed a treasure of historical information. The huge amount of information I acquired from my parents and relatives—who had no idea why I interviewed them—felt overpowering. I might say they were honored and glad to share all with me, and even applauded me, saying that nobody was previously so concerned about family history.

I am proud to document the history of my family, and it is now transmittable from generation to generation, as he says in Psalms 125:4, 'One generation shall commend your work in another, and shall declare your mighty acts." I also understand better who I am and on a deeper level because of my awareness of my legacy and the origins of my life. It all enabled me to shape my identity.

Yet our identity is more than our legacy or our names. I believe our identity starts with knowledge and consciousness. Then, as we travel around the world, the structure we call "ourselves" becomes a combination of our significant mental characteristics, relationships we form, and all that takes place in our lives; all these elements create our individualism, our identity, and how we manifest ourselves in our lives. The more I investigated the origins of identity, the more I realized I no longer wanted to fuse with the socialist values and aspirations I saw in this "fallen" world. Why can't I fan the fire the Creator breathed into me and carry it through my life? I just knew that I no longer wanted to live my life with regret, humiliation, or sadness for not knowing who I was. The more we can understand our identity, the more we may feel love for ourselves and the others around us.

Traditionally, from a broader perspective, I recognize that each one of us is a result of our social contacts and conscious activities across the world. Strengthening the social character of the person is ordinary and even normal; its emergence and growth are only possible thanks to living in society. The world we live in, as well as our choices and relationships, all form who we are and how we live. It is also crucial to acknowledge the value of where we came from. It is a gift to know our history, so we can transmit our legacy.

Now, I'm on the quest of keeping my family values and dreams alive and passing them on to my children. I'm going to do it. I will! I promised my Grandpa Garegin of Armenia! It is up to us to protect our heritage. When we do, we plunge deeper into our identities. In return, we plunge deeper into our connection with God.

Questions To Consider

- When you decide where you are going to search for answers, are you rooting your search in your faith?
- Our legacy is part and parcel of who we are. Have you ever wondered where your relatives are from? Find an elderly relative and ask them to share your family history with you. How does it make you feel after you hear it?

Chapter Seven

THE VALUES IN YOUR LIFE

"When your values are clear to you, making decisions becomes easier."
– Roy E. Disney

As a leader, it is vital to realize, to grasp what "value" in life implies, because everyone living on this planet has their own set of distinctive values. Each person has his distinctive moments and is independent of anyone else. So, it is hard to tell everyone exactly what "value" means; each one of us has our unique circumstances, which constitute our personal lives, and which establish our distinctive values.

This chapter reflects the ideals I have found in my own life. It is very important to me that I recall my values every day I am alive, whether the day was easy or hard, bad or wonderful. Every minute, something exceptional might happen that might fundamentally transform my life. Some individuals spend their days and lives ungratefully thinking to themselves, "There's always tomorrow." I don't think that's appropriate. I think we have to live every minute of every day. God gave us life to enjoy and to savor every minute He gave us.

This is His gift to us, and why Jesus died on the cross, that we might live. Ecclesiastes 3:1 reminds us: "There is an occasion for everything and a time for every activity under heaven." The value of life lies not only in our life's moments, but also in the people in our hearts. First, we have to value our parents who have given us life because we have been able to achieve a feeling of freedom and happiness from them. Yet, in addition to our parents, we can't forget to cherish the people around us who stood up and provided a bright light for us; our lives would have a dark streak without them. Finally, if we were so fortunate that we had children, then we value them, because our lives would be meaningless without them. For many, like me, family and those near to us is the the vast majority of what we cherish.

I unearthed more jewels when I went into my value system. I find it necessary for me not to interfere with others, but to live my life with dignity; to try to identify common ground; to think about the excellent things and look for the best in all; to uplift the spirit of each person whenever I have the chance. Remember that everybody has a nice side, although it may sometimes be difficult to see.

I recognized that comparison was a waste of time. I had to be careful that my tenacity may interfere with resolving some of my past hurts. I have learned it is crucial to name our ideals, for it is the cornerstone of our honesty. Proverbs 10:9 further adds, "Whoever walks in integrity walks securely, but he who makes his way crooked will be found out."

Only one life is given to each of us, which is the most significant gift we will ever receive. We would not exist without it. It is, therefore, crucial that we acknowledge God's gift of life by moderating our strength and stability of character. Most essentially, we must safeguard all life on Earth and never forget to care for our little siblings, and finally, to live in a way that we are never embarrassed by.

The longer we live, the more we look back at how we lived our years. We don't want to look back with regret; every hour we must feel and live as if it's our last and take care of our dear ones. The world is full of friendly and helpful people. It is also full of intriguing and unusual people. Not everyone in life is who we are and what we value, thus the views of people around us must be respected. If we were not to waste our talent and try to achieve perfection and work towards positive results and correct solutions, life would not be as complete. Take care of your loved ones, aid your parents. The closer I looked at my list of values and identified with it, the more I saw and wrote it down. The more I found out who I was and understood my identity.

Everything in life always changes. A life of value is the only life to live. It's the present. With time, we can maybe begin to realize more, that everything around us is independent of us—yet connected, nonetheless. If we want to grasp what we live for—*why* we live—we can get up early and start praying and thank the Lord for our lives. This kind of prayer gets us to our knees in thanks, provides value, and offers us more to accomplish than merely spending another day passing time. It gives us life—a life full of the breath of God, as Jobs 33:4 says, "The spirit of God has made me, and the breath of the Almighty gives me life."

"To thrive, to feel the breath of God and the Spirit of God in my nose all good things must overpower the negative in life" (Job 27:3). A leader has to continue ahead and not give up!

Questions To Consider

- What does "value" mean to you? Do you know your essential values?
- Who do you appreciate in your life? Does somebody you care about need to hear from you, so they know how valuable they are?
- How can you find more value in your day and be grateful every hour? Make it your practice today in faith.

Chapter Eight

LEARNING TO CONCENTRATE WITH YOUR EYES

"It's not what you look at that matters, it's what you see."
– Henry David Thoreau

I remember when my parents dropped me at daycare in the summer. There was a particular tree in the beautiful garden that I admired. I would sit under it, exchanging thoughts and emotions. It had a long, dead branch at the bottom on the trunk. Like any beautiful thing, there was an element we had to avoid that looked "forbidden" or "hidden".

In my family, we often say, "There are demons in a tranquil pool," which means that not everyone who looked humble and serene really was. There's another metaphor I like to use about a pond. A pond often has a swirling counter-current. The strength of the pool is concealed by its perceived tranquility. However, in this tranquility, in these images, devils are found, dull and strange. It's a precipice, a terror, darkness, a frigid abyss, danger, and death.

They caution us against the disappointment of humility and seeming complacency. For example, in Greece, they say, "Keep a tranquil river, not a stormy one." The British say this as "quiet, deep waters". The French warn, "There is nothing worse than the sleeping water." It is usual in Spain to say of illusory calmness, "Quiet water is harmful." Italians claim, "Quiet water destroys bridges," and Poles believe, "Calm water is washing the beach." The treason of tranquil water, to the Slavs, is intimately linked to the wicked spirits who live there. Ukrainian and Belarusian proverbs and Russians say, "Devils breed in a peaceful marsh."

Acts of Temptations

There are always temptations and self-disappointments in life—if we base our decisions on the opinions of others. Temptations are tied to the future, and since it is frequently hard for individuals to focus on the present out of fear of their dreams; it is simpler to live on fantasy than to face up to the duty we have at present. That can lead to even more self-disappointment, which leads to misunderstandings of love, relationships, and trust. As 1 John 4:1 says, "Blessed are you; do not believe every spirit, but test the spirits, to see if they are of God, since many false prophets have gone into the world."

One summer day, a five-year-old boy played with his soccer ball near my tree. He was so preoccupied with the pleasure of kicking and chasing the ball that he didn't notice his own strength. It landed under my giant tree when he kicked it over his friend's head. He chased his ball. As he ran toward the tree, my heart began to race, and my body shook. I yelled for him to stop, but he didn't hear me. I knew if he didn't stop the low branch, it would smash directly into his eye or forehead, damaging him for life.

In my life, I had never run so quickly. I had to stop the boy from getting hurt. The branch that was destined to enter the boy's eye, entered mine instead, completely destroying it. I felt the worst pain I've ever felt, suffering resulting from my innocent, noble action to help someone else.

My dreams failed. It crushed my confidence and optimism and stole my delight forever. I was devastated. It was my heart that ached the most, more than my sight. My tree had deceived me.

Essence of our Sight

Sensory perceptions can destroy anyone who finds it difficult to survive. It can lead to the loss of critical thinking between who we are and what we think as human beings—and our feelings. As a result, we may stop understanding what is happening. I believe people can formulate plans and want to set them into action—plans that aren't necessarily healthy or wise. Yet, they come to their senses, seeing the impact and consequences of their actions before it's too late. I, on the other hand, hadn't come to my senses—at least not in time and not before major damage was done to my eye.

Reaity World

I had stopped assessing the situation adequately. My perceptions of what was happening at this time were deeply connected with my subconscious, and I couldn't see the truth. The agony I suffered was both internal and an exterior. Often, we want our identity to rest on the people we love. We look for love and dream about love. We paint magnificent, bright images in our minds that cannot coexist with our reality. We hide from each other to feel better and to create false realities. Life feels too painful sometimes to look directly in the eye. Here, though, I experienced the worst pain I'd ever felt, due to my own conduct and a tree I loved profoundly. I will never forget the day or the tree. The tree impressed me greatly, and I learned something essential from it.

Our memory is a wonderful power that holds in our minds both the beautiful and horrendous events that captured our attention and became part of all that made us who we now are. Our recollections might be linked to art or music. Even in nature, feelings and memories can awaken. Remembrances help us live, dream, and hope for the best. Memories can have pure colors and brilliant tones filling us with joy, as we remember the unique event in our lives. Memories can linger within us for an eternity, and it's like a slice of life when they surface. It's a beauty that opens before our eyes.

Building Memories

I'm asking my tree now! How do you want me to remember you? It was not an easy day for me to be hurt by the tree. I could barely see through my remaining eye, which was coated with blood.

I held to the words of my father like an anchor when he assured me everything would be okay. I knew he *wasn't* sure of my recovery, yet with all my heart, I believed him. I knew my father wasn't able to lie. I had no reason to doubt it. I had to trust by faith that God was going to work through the medicines the doctor had given us to heal my eye. I was brought back to the Bible verses, Isaiah 41:10: "Therefore, do not be afraid, for I am with you; don't be frightened, because I am your God. I will strengthen you and help you. With my righteous right hand, I will uphold you."

Questions To Consider

- Have you ever seen a scenario one way, and then afterward, realized that was the wrong way to see it? If so, how long did it take you to realize that?

Chapter Nine

YOUR INNER EYE'S WINDOW

"Doubt your doubts before you doubt your faith."
– President Dieter F. Uchtdorf

As leaders, we must understand our inner eye's window. At such a young age, my experience with nearly losing sight helped me cherish the gift of seeing. It's funny that the tree I adored for its beauty had almost taken away my ability to enjoy nature fully. Physical vision is very important—just look around this beautiful world!. Yet, what if we could see, but couldn't *really* see? The depth of who we are goes much farther than what we take in with our physical senses. You have, perhaps, heard the classic quotation, "The eyes are the window to the soul." What is deep within us can shine through our eyes and reveal the depth of who we are.

This is where vision transcends the physical understanding of all that happens to us in our lives. Our search for meaning leads us to a wisdom we might not have found if we hadn't searched. Yet, God created the world for our appreciation and enjoyment, as stated in Psalm 118:23: "This is the Lord's doing; it is marvelous in our eyes."

My eyes and what I perceive give me joy—through my eyes. I like to observe the first sparkles of the new day's emergence. The sun proclaims its approach well before it rises in the east. He adorns the night sky with his rays and extinguishes the morning. I enjoy meeting the sun and morning delight, the bursts of its rays.

First, the horizon shows a fiery red streak. Then, the sun fills all around and becomes orange and pink. And as though I first saw a green leaf, a tree which waxed to my window, and a bright nebula settled over my hometown, waking up to this new day. The dawn delivers a new day, full of the responsibilities of life and a gentle, "Good morning!"

To the extent that we may enjoy and appreciate the outside world God made, our fundamental wants originate from the spiritual world of man. The spiritual world, the realm of his thoughts and feelings, is the interior world of man. Imagine there was a fairy kingdom within each one of us, termed an inner realm; a land invisible to our eyes, but we undoubtedly know it exists. Like any kingdom, there is a King, who has numerous servants and subjects, who revere him. These servants and subjects symbolize our sentiments, thoughts, possibilities, skills, and more.

Our Inner World

Those subjects were usually prepared at the first request of the King to come to his help, since all the Kingdom's inhabitants respected the king for his wisdom, his justice, his love, his kindness, and his concern for his people. You may ask, who, then, in our inner world is the wise ruler? The King is our thoughts, our conscience. At all times, our inner monarch thinks about what's best for us. If our leader is strong, intelligent, and kind, we may achieve a great deal in our life; if he is weak and faint, life will be hard. Those with weak rulers generally don't handle their feelings effectively, and change their mood often. They don't know what they want – one thing today and another tomorrow, which are sometimes contrary. It is not possible to be friends with persons whose internal discipline is faint and sluggish; usually, they are difficult to satisfy, temperamental, or irritated. This is how much depends on our inner king's authority.

We need to explore our inner kingdom and spiritual realm. In this way, we can expand our King's power. After all, the person who knows what he is doing is much stronger and more knowledgeable than the person who doesn't know even what country he has. We can gaze beyond the external appearance if we keep the eyes of our hearts and souls open. Only then will we start to pay attention to our inner world beyond the exterior world around us. 2 Corinthians 10:7 sets us back on track in the proper direction. "You see things as they are externally. If someone trusts in himself that he is Christ's, let him consider that in himself, as He is Christ's, we too are."

Questions To Consider

- What do you think is the difference between internal vision and external vision? Do you believe you ought to live your life and see your life through God's eyes?
- Name a memory that gives you comfort or a time you learned something significant in your life.

Chapter Ten

BE KIND TO OTHERS

"There is no better spiritual exercise as a leader than reaching down and lifting people."

The Bible says, "and be ye kind one to another" (Ephesians 4:32). Kindness, in my opinion, is frequently associated with spending money or doing something extraordinary. But being kind goes much deeper than that. I firmly believe that simple or small acts of kindness have a greater impact on others. God commanded us to be kind one to another because, while being kind is beneficial to others, it also improves your own well-being. Kindness increases satisfaction, decreases pain, and even improves your health. Just a few kind acts per week can help you live a longer, happier life, by reducing stress.

Being kind is an important way to give our lives meaning. It also brightens the lives of those around us. Being kind enables us to communicate more effectively, be more compassionate, and positively influence people's lives. Kindness comes from deep within you, and while some people are born with it, it is something that everyone can learn by choice.

The words of Ephesians 4:32 are tangible evidence of Paul's kindness to others through the wisdom and Spirit of God. As it is stated, "Be kind and compassionate to one another, forgiving each other, just as in Christ, God forgave you."

We are asked to be kind and sympathetic. Why must the passage of the Bible remind us to be kind to one another? Is there a special reason for God's command? Let us analyze Paul's passage to find out why God requires us to be kind, forgiving, and compassionate.

Because God is Kind

The Bible says we should be kind to one another because God is kind to us. In Ephesians 4:32, it is first mentioned to be kind. This is because Paul specifically says that the church at Ephesus is kind and focuses not only on helping, but on being kind to all.

We might also read other chapters in the Bible that urge us to be friendly. In Galatians 5:22 it is written, "But the fruit of the Spirit is love, joy, peace, forbearance, kindness, goodness, faithfulness." Kindness is included here alongside love, happiness, peace, endurance, goodness, and faithfulness as the fruit of the Spirit. This means God has given us a very essential gift that we must use; a path we must follow because Jesus Christ, Himself, possesses all these characteristics.

Jesus Christ is kind to the reader of the Bible, especially in Matthew 8:1-4, when Jesus cures a leper. It is written: When Jesus came down from the mountainside, large crowds followed him. A man with leprosy came and knelt before him and said, "Lord, if you are willing, you can make me clean."

Jesus touched the man and reached out his hand. "I'm willing," he said. "Be pure!" He was rid of his leprosy immediately. Then, Jesus told him, "See you don't tell anyone. But go and show yourself to the priest and give them the gift which Moses instructed."

In this verse, we can easily imagine the character of Jesus and His kindness. We, too, ought to be the same. We should be willing, even when they are not kind to us, to be kind to our neighbors. In our daily deeds, we should demonstrate a character precisely like our Lord Jesus Christ, because God, Himself, is compassionate and tender.

Paul also tells us to be compassionate in Ephesians 4:32. In the original language, it employs the Greek term *eusplanchnoi*, meaning "strong-hearted", or "compassionate", or "tender-hearted". The verse focuses on the concept of sympathy in which Paul tells the faithful not to be harsh, because Jesus Christ is a gentle and compassionate teacher.

This is also shown in the Good Samaritan parable, in which Jesus Christ tells a story of an individual who is caring and has no limits, who does not care about race or political affiliation. In Luke 10:25-37, it is written that on one occasion, an expert in the law stood up to test Jesus. "Teacher," he asked, "what must I do to inherit eternal life?"

"What is written in the Law?" he replied. "How do you read it?" He answered, "'Love the Lord your God with all your heart and with all your soul and with all your strength and with all your mind;' and, 'Love your neighbor as yourself.'"

"You have answered correctly," Jesus replied. "Do this, and you will live." But he wanted to justify himself, so he asked Jesus, "And who is my neighbor?"

In reply, Jesus said: "A man was going down from Jerusalem to Jericho when he was attacked by robbers. They stripped him of his clothes, beat him, and went away, leaving him half-dead. A priest happened to be going down the same road, and when he saw the man, he passed by on the other side. So too, a Levite, when he came to the place and saw him, passed by on the other side. But a Samaritan, as he traveled, came where the man was; and when he saw him, he took pity on him. He went to him.

"Which of these three do you believe was the man's neighbor who fell into thieves' hands?" The law expert answered, "The one who felt compassion for him." Jesus said to him, "Go and do the same."

Sometimes, there is a lack of compassion in the world. There are no "good Samaritans". We see a person who needs assistance, and we turn a blind eye. The Word of God always urges us to be kind by being sympathetic. If someone needs support, emotionally or physically, it is our Christian obligation to be nice and help. No matter how tiny or large our kindness may be, all kindness has the same face. We must demonstrate sympathy and compassion in every way we can.

Because God Forgives

Also, to be kind implies showing forgiveness. Paul orders us to forgive, as it is written in Ephesians 4:32. Why? Because it fulfills the mandate of a God who forgives. The forgiveness of God is beyond this world. Imagine sending His only begotten Son into the world of sinners and saving them from eternal damnation by forgiving them their crimes. Matthew 6:12 reminds us of the remission of God, "And forgive us our debts, as we also have forgiven our debtors."

We read many verses in the Bible about forgiveness. It is said in Matthew 18:21-35: "Then Peter came to Jesus, and said, 'Lord, how often should I forgive my brother or sister who is sinful to me? Up to seven times?'

Jesus answered, 'I tell you, not seven times, but seventy-seven times.'"

"Therefore, the kingdom of heaven is like a king who wanted to settle accounts with his servants. As he began the settlement, a man who owed him ten thousand bags of gold was brought to him. Since he was not able to pay, the master ordered that he and his wife and his children and all he had be sold to repay the debt. "At this, the servant fell on his knees before him. 'Be patient with me,' he begged, 'and I will pay back everything.' The servant's master took pity on him, canceled the debt, and let him go.

"But when that servant went out, he found one of his fellow servants who owed him a hundred silver coins. He grabbed him and began to choke him. 'Pay back what you owe me!' he demanded. "His fellow servant fell to his knees and begged him, 'Be patient with me, and I will pay it back.'

"But he refused. Instead, he went off and had the man thrown into prison until he could pay the debt. When the other servants saw what had happened, they were outraged and went and told their master everything that had happened. Then the master called the servant in. 'You wicked servant,' he said, 'I canceled all that debt of yours because you begged me to. Shouldn't you have had mercy on your fellow servant just as I had on you?' In anger, his master handed him over to the jailers to be tortured until he should pay back all he owed.

"This is how my heavenly Father will treat each of you, unless you forgive your brother or sister from your heart."

We might imagine in these verses that Jesus tells His followers how to forgive, and it is boundless. However, it is sometimes quite difficult to forgive, especially those who hurt us. The Bible teaches us that compassion involves pardoning, no matter how big a person's error is. It is our Christian responsibility to forgive, since the Father forgives.

Why Is This Important

As leaders, the Bible tells us to be kind to each other, because our God is kind to us. He commanded us through Paul's words to be kind, sympathetic, and forgiving. Therefore, as servant leaders, we must follow.

Questions To Consider

- How do you treat those who can do nothing for you in return?
- Are you glad when others succeed?
- How do you deal with others in times of crisis?

My Final Thoughts

Each one of us here today has had our own challenges—and our own unique dreams. But the one dream I know we have in common is that each one of us wants to make a difference in the world *and create value*—and today marks a very important day where we are on the way to doing just that. We are the change-makers.

Each one of you has reached for the impossible and achieved it; has made an effort, worked hard, and held onto your dreams and never given up. With God by your side, you took action to bring your dream into reality. You are victorious!

I am an immigrant and direct descendant of an Armenian genocide survivor. My great-grandfather, despite witnessing his parents being beheaded in front of his eyes, still carried out his dream to create a generation of people with vision—survivors, victors, and builders of their dreams. I have fought and conquered many personal battles. My dad did not want me when he found out his first-born was a girl. I was rejected by my grandparents, because I did not look like them. I was called ugly by my relatives, since I did not resemble them in the color of my skin, hair, and eyes. I was turned down from Georgian universities because of my Russian last name. But by God's grace, He moved me through these hurdles. My dad and I have a loving, close relationship, and he sees my value. My grandparents accept me and love me. I entered a beauty pageant in which I won the title of People's Choice Award Winner, despite rigged judging. And I became the only one from my country to study abroad with a full scholarship.

Power of Dreams

Through my journey, what I've discovered is that when we hold God's hand and allow Him to fill us with the strength to overcome what we believe are *insurmountable* obstacles—when we push through in faith, no matter how hard it may feel, we crack something open inside of ourselves that allows our hearts to open and our dreams to truly come alive.

Dreaming is our ticket to the future. Without dreaming about the future, we wouldn't take action today. Ralph Waldo Emerson once wrote, "*What lies behind us and what lies in front of us pales in comparison to what lies within us.*" If I have learned anything, it's that there is no secret formula to achieve success. But it does require a deep-seated passion, a burning desire to strive for what rings true to the person you are, and to DREAM it into reality.

May your trials always lead to opportunities, and may the hope of God always fill you with the joy and peace.

God is by Your Side

Oftentimes, life feels messy. Many times, it feels challenging. Life can be scary. Yet, that's what makes our dreams that much more precious when they arrive, which is always on God's timing. Our dreams are held in God's arms. As it says in Habakkuk 2:2-3: "And the Lord answered me: 'Write the vision; make it plain on tablets, so he may run who reads it. For still the vision awaits its appointed time; it hastens to the end—it will not lie. If it seems slow, wait for it; it will surely come; it will not delay.'"

Today, I feel humbled to share these pages with victorious change-makers. Lastly, please remember YOU are the dream-maker of your life, and God stands proud beside you. He supports you when you fall. He cheers you on when you are victorious.

Chapter Eleven

YOU ARE GOD'S SERVANT

Leaders Serve

God is the creator of all things. And, as a leader in your community, you are God's servant.

As a leader in your community, you are truly God's servant. Always remember, God is the creator of all things, and God has a purpose for your life. Oftentimes, individuals find themselves drifting throughout life, and it isn't until a major event or a tragic event or a challenge or a trial or tribulation occurs in someone's life that they then awaken to understand God's purpose for their life.

Serve From a Full Cup, not an Empty Cup

As God's children and as leaders in our community, we are truly God's servants. And, as God's servants, we are called to lead his people. God wants us to serve his people, no matter what. Therefore, as God's servant, it is very important to make sure that your cup is filled, because you cannot serve people from an empty cup. Therefore, always take the time to make sure that your cup is filled.

It's Not About you, It's About Serving Others

Always remember: it's not about you anymore; it's about serving others. Sometimes, that requires that you realize you need to take yourself out of the equation. That's right: take yourself out of the equation and focus on serving his people. And, wherever you show up to serve, make sure you serve and provide value to others. Don't just show up to show up. When you show up, show up and serve and provide value, no matter what.

Fill In the Blank:

1. Are you a leader in your community?
   _____

2. Do you understand that as a leader in your community, you are God's servant?
   _____

3. Is your cup filled, or do you find yourself serving from an empty cup?
   _____

4. Do you understand that it is not about you, and it is about serving others?
   _____

5. How are you serving others in your community?
   _____

6. What is one thing that you can do this year to help someone else?
   _____

Chapter Twelve

YOU ARE NOT ALONE ON YOUR LIFE JOURNEY

God is with you wherever you go

"Have I not commanded you? Be strong and courageous. Do not be afraid; do not be discouraged, for the Lord, your God, will be with you wherever you go."- Joshua 1:9

Therefore, always remember God is with you wherever you go; you are not alone.

No matter what trial, tribulation, or challenge you may have faced in your life—and you may feel alone after the fact—remember: you are not alone. God is with you, as it states in the Bible. And, if you can have faith as small as a mustard seed, you will realize that no matter what trial, tribulation, or challenge you face in your life, you, too, can overcome, no matter what. No matter what you go through in this lifetime, it is all in the mindset. Mindset is a very powerful thing, and once you realize that, you can overcome anything. If you ever find yourself in a negative state of mind, shift your mindset from a negative mindset to a positive mindset and maintain it.

You Have Support from Your Community

Now, also remember you are not alone because you have support from your community. No matter what you go through, you will one day realize, if you haven't already, your community is there to support you, no matter what.

I share this story with you. A woman had gone through a traumatic event in regard to domestic violence and she almost lost her life, which would have been ruled death by strangulation. She was able to recover because of the support not just from God, her family, or friends, but from her community. Therefore, when we talk about community, it is very important to understand that support from your community—such as in that case, a domestic violence advocate, who supported the woman—can be integral. Once you realize that you have full support from your community, just like understanding that God is with you wherever you go, there is nothing that you can't overcome—nothing. How do I know this? Because that woman is me. Yes, you read that right. I am a domestic violence survivor. Here I am before you today, because of the support from God and understanding that God is with me wherever I go, as well as receiving full support from my family, friends, and our community.

I am here to tell you that no matter what you have been through, you, too, can overcome and remember, God is with you wherever you go, and again, you have full support from your community. Never give up. Keep moving forward, no matter what.

Fill In the Blank

1. When do you feel alone?

2. What is one thing that you can do today, so that you don't feel alone?
   _____

3. 3) What is your state of mind right now, and what can you do to change it?
   _____

4. Do you understand that you have full support from your community?
   _____

5. Tell me a time where your community supported you?
   _____

6. Where are you now on your life journey?
   _____

Chapter Thirteen

YOU CAN OVERCOME THE CHALLENGES IN YOUR LIFE

God First

It is so important now more than ever for folks to understand the importance of having God in first place in their lives. We would not have all the issues that we have in society if people were to keep God in his proper place, which is first.

There have been so many leaders before us, such as Bill Bright, Brad Bright, and Billy Graham who have tried to tell us one thing: to keep God first in our lives. With so many leaders such as them trying to tell us this, why is it that in the large society that we live in today, that God first is not spoken about enough? Why?

Why is there a stigma attached to speaking about God? Why is God first not taught in our education system? In a manner of which, we can respect each other's religious views. The time has come now in our generation when we should be able to have a classroom on religion or God, where everyone can respect the topic at hand in regard to a higher power.

Now, I am not saying for anyone to compromise, but what I am saying is for people to be open-minded to the topic of religion being an open discussion. Where people don't attack each other verbally and people can respect each other's views. It's not complex; it is simply respecting each other. The time has come now, where we as a society can do so, but it starts with us as royal warriors on the front lines, to help others understand the importance of this transition in our generation, because where we are going as society, one day religion will be discussed openly, and it is key to remember that whomever you believe in— Higher Power/ God first—it is always important to keep God first in your life, no matter what. With God First in your life, there is truly no challenge that you cannot overcome.

You hear stories all the time about people telling you that they had a major challenge in their lives, but have you ever stopped to ask someone, what got you through? If you haven't done that yet, take time the next time someone tells you that they have been through a major challenge. Ask them, what got you through? It is at that very moment that you will realize, it is their faith that got them through. God first.

Resilient Mindset

It is also very important to maintain a resilient mindset. A resilient mindset is your ability to bounce back after a major challenge has occurred in your life, no matter what. That means it doesn't matter how many times you fall down, whether you fall down in life or in business, you get back up, no matter what.

The enemy will always try to attack, but as long as you have the right mindset and you understand God's purpose for your life, there is nothing you can't overcome. With faith and with the right mindset—that is, a resilient mindset—there is no challenge that you can't overcome.

Take a moment now to pause and think about a time where you had a major challenge in your life, and now I ask you: what got you through? It was your faith, wasn't it? Therefore, always remember that it is very important not just to keep God first when a major challenge happens or afterwards, but every day of your life. Every day that you are breathing on this earth, keep Him first, no matter what. And remember: when you get quiet, you can hear Him and you can listen to Him, because it doesn't matter how many plans you make, God directs your steps. Whether you believe it or not, He is the creator of all things; no one got here by accident—He knew in His vision and in His mind how He was going to form you and what he needed you to do on this earth to serve his people.

Once you come in alignment with purpose, you are unstoppable. As a royal warrior on the front line, you have a duty as God's servant to make sure that no matter what challenge you are faced with in your life, you keep God first, maintain a resilient mindset, and get through, so that you can continue to serve his people. Lead by example, walk by faith and not by sight.

Fill In the Blank

1. What is a major challenge that occurred in your life?
   _____

2. Do you have God first in your life?
   _____

3. Do you understand what a resilient mindset is?
   _____

4. Is God in your life and business?

   _____

5. Tell me another time where your faith got you through a major challenge.

   _____

6. Do you read the Bible daily?

   _____

Chapter Fourteen

YOU ARE A LEADER WHO IS A ROYAL WARRIOR

Royal Warrior Defined

You are a royal warrior. That's right: you are a royal warrior, and as a royal warrior, you are on the front lines. Now, what does it truly mean to be a royal warrior?

We're not talking about being fancy and just sitting on the front lines doing nothing; what we mean is that you are enough, you are worthy of being God's servant, and He has a purpose for your life. As a leader, you are a royal warrior, because you are going to have so many trials, tribulations, and challenges to overcome in your life, but no matter what, you need to keep getting back up, and keep up the good fight, because when you keep up the good fight, you can help someone else. There are so many people who need your help, who need a helping hand to lift them up. Sometimes, just by hearing your story, you can get them through, because you are someone else's hope.

Royal Warriors Never Give Up

It is so important that you don't give up, because if you give up, that's it: you let the enemy win. If you give up, you will go into depression, you have anxiety, you live in fear, and you have all of these negative aspects in your life that you shouldn't have in your life, because life is a beautiful thing. When you only see your circumstance, then that's it: you will only live in your circumstance. If you can be in your circumstance and see beyond the matter at hand, then you can truly live God's purpose for your life.

Understand that a moment is just a moment, and no matter what you are going through right now, this, too, shall pass. One day, your surroundings, your circumstance, will no longer be there. Days pass, months pass, years pass, time passes, so what you see today is not your tomorrow. Therefore, what you do in the now, in this moment, every single day with blood, sweat, and tears, that is going to be your future. You are writing your story as we speak. Every single day you wake up, you are creating your future, so what are you doing every single day? That's right, what are you doing every single day? What you do today determines your tomorrow.

If you give up now, then that's it: you have no future. That's right: you have no future if you give up now, but if you get up every single day and you work hard, and you continue to build, what eventually happens? For example, if a contractor continues to build, build, and build, brick by brick, brick by brick, and they are adding bricks to build a building, what happens? What is the end result? The end result is the contractor has built a beautiful building. It might take a few months or years to build that building, but it's not the time that matters; what matters is that they never gave up. Now, if they gave up, the end result would not be a beautiful building. What you would get is just sitting bricks, but if you can move the pieces and put them together, what you get at the end is a beautiful building.

No matter what you are going through in life right now, understand you are the contractor of your life. What are you building every single day? If you have given up, I highly recommend rethinking why you gave up. Why did you give up so soon? Rethink. Get back up, because the fight isn't over. You are just a contractor who may have some bricks sitting around, but they are still there. If something caused you to have to put the brick down, understand you have an alternative. There is always an alternative. There is still an alternative way to get the brick up; you just have to find the solution. There is always a solution to a problem. Yes, it's just like math. You can never have a math equation without a solution— there is always an end result.

What is one equation in your life that you have not figured out the solution for yet? Remember that you still have time on this earth, while you are still breathing, to find that solution, find that alternative if needed, but no matter what, by any means necessary, get back up, and keep building, brick by brick, because the end result will be a beautiful result. Remember: growth is truly the beauty of life. Keep growing and continuing to learn, because when you continue to learn, you continue to grow. Never give up.

Fill In the Blank

1. What is a royal warrior?
   _____

2. Are you ready to be on the front lines as a royal warrior?
   _____

3. What is a gold that you are looking to achieve in your life?

   _____

4. Do you understand that you need to have the mindset of never giving up?

   _____

Chapter Fifteen

BE COURAGEOUS!

Face Your Challenges

Take a moment right now. What does it truly mean to be courageous? To be courageous means that no matter what, you face everything head on, everything in this lifetime, which requires that you don't have depression, you don't have anxiety, and you don't live in fear. That's right: a lot of those things are keeping people down, but not you, because you see, when you can overcome all of those things, you can help someone else overcome them, to be courageous, no matter what. Always remember, in this lifetime, you need to face your challenges.

Facing your challenges means that no matter what occurs in your life, you are able to acknowledge that it happened, because once you acknowledge that the challenge occurred, then you can overcome the challenge.

A lot of folks tend to avoid the challenges that occur in their lives, because of fear, anxiety, or depression, so what happens is they continue to drift in their lives, but not you, because you are a royal warrior, and it required if you are going to be on the front lines, to be courageous and face your challenges. I faced being sexually assaulted as a child and as an adult, so if I can overcome that, then you can overcome anything in your life.

There is a gentleman, and that gentleman had a boating accident, and in his boating accident, he lost one of his arms at a very young age, but you see where he could've just lived in fear, or been ruled by anxiety or depression, what he did was face his challenges. He faced that challenge, he acknowledged that he lost his arm in a boating accident. He acknowledged that his left arm was amputated. And, when he acknowledged that his arm was amputated, it is at that very moment that he was able to build the confidence to face his challenge, and he then shifted his mindset from a negative mindset to a positive mindset, to then be able to become one of the greatest personal trainers of the world today.

Now, as a royal warrior on the front lines, he gives back to his community. With just one arm, he is a personal trainer at a well-known gym franchise. If he can do it, you can overcome any challenge. And remember: to overcome any challenge, it first starts with you facing the challenge.

Joshua 1:9

"Have I not commanded you? Be strong and courageous. Do not be afraid; do not be discouraged, for the Lord, your God, will be with you wherever you go."

Fill In the Blank

1. Are you courageous?
   _____

2. What is a challenge you need to face in your life?
   _____

3. Tell me a story of someone you know who has faced their challenge.
   _____

4. Do you understand that it is required to face your challenge in order to be on the front lines?
   _____

Chapter Sixteen

ACHIEVE YOUR GOALS

"Action"

It is very important in this lifetime to realize that when you set a goal, you need to achieve each and every one of them. It doesn't matter if there is a delay or detour, when you set a goal, you need to accomplish it.

In this lifetime, there may be something external that keeps you from achieving your goal in the moment, but that is just a moment, and that moment shall pass. It's not the moment that matters— it is about what you do after the fact, after the incident occurs. What are you going to do? You can still achieve your goal; it's all a matter of mindset and finding the alternative, because as I previously stated, there is always an alternative to achieving a goal, but if you can stay focused on achieving a specific goal, then you can overcome anything.

> *"You can set a goal. However, in order to achieve a goal, action is required."*
> *- **Regeline Eden Sabbat***

God knows the plans He has for you. God will not bring you to anything He can't get you through.

You may set a goal, and you may have a clear vision for what you want, but God may cause a delay or detour on your journey and then still get you to your goal in the future, but what may happen is you may not understand now why God caused a delay or detour, but when you eventually achieve your goal, what you are going to realize is that God wanted to give you something bigger. Something bigger than you could have ever imagined. When you see a goal, God sees a bigger goal. God sees that same goal and vision that you are looking to do, because He put it in your mind, but understand that God has something bigger for you that he didn't want you to foresee yet, because He wanted to gift that to you.

Therefore, when you set a goal, often, the end result is bigger than you could have ever imagined, but thank God for that blessing, because it is a blessing in disguise, which means that He is gifting you something. That means that God has something for you that cannot be seen yet, but if you have faith as small as a mustard seed, once you achieve your goal, you will see what God had for you is bigger than you could have ever imagined.

Fill In the Blank

1. What is something that you need to let go and let God?
   _____

2. Do you understand that God is control?
   _____

3. What is a goal that you have yet to take action on?

   _____

4. Do you understand in order to achieve a goal, action is required?

   _____

Chapter Seventeen

BE EFFECTIVE IN WHAT YOU DO

Leadership

As a leader in your community, when you show up, you need to serve and provide value. Don't be a leader who shows up and doesn't provide value. Don't show up just to show up, because it is unacceptable.

As a leader, give back to your community. You have the skills and the knowledge to serve God's people. Therefore, give back. God doesn't bring you through life just to bring you through life, so you can sit back and have a great time—no, He brings through all the experiences that you have been through, so that eventually, one day, you can give back and serve His people.

Therefore, it is very important for you to realize, that as a royal warrior, you are on the front lines, and when you are on the front lines, it is a daily battle, because what you are dealing with is the enemy on the other side, and that enemy is negativity.

Every single day that you breathe on this earth, you may come across a negative aspect/factor in your life, but understand you have control of your mind and how you perceive things, and how you handle each matter. For example, you can let it be processed in your mind and affect your mood and your day, or you can just acknowledge that it happened and move forward and maintain a positive mindset, so that you can go on with your day and handle what you need to do. If you don't nip that in the bud in that moment, what is going to happen is that you are going to be in a negative state of mind, and you are not going to be an effective leader. Again, remember you cannot lead from an empty cup, so if you let negative factors affect your life or your mood as a leader, when you show up to serve, then you cannot be effective in what you do. Therefore, as a leader, it is required that you have full control of your emotions. Emotional intelligence is a key component of being a leader.

Fill In the Blank

1. Do you understand what emotional intelligence is?
   _____

2. What does leadership mean to you?
   _____

3. Are you a leader in your community?
   _____

4. Are you being effective in what you do?
   _____

Chapter Eighteen

LIVE YOUR DREAMS

Stop Drifting in Your Life

Stop drifting. Enough is enough. Too often, folks just drift through life. Have you ever heard someone say," I wish I knew then what I know now," or, "I am too old to do that now," or, "I can't do that now." Those are all examples of someone who is drifting through life.

Time is going to pass anyway, but what are you going to do with your time?

Time is very valuable. If you don't want to be in the future asking yourself what if, then what you do right now in the present moment is very important, because you are only given one life. You don't get to have 20 years pass by just doing nothing, and then later on be able to say, "Let me go back and see what can be done." No, you don't get another lifetime— you only get one.

What are you going to do differently today, to make sure you have a better tomorrow? As a leader, when you handle what you need to do, then you can help someone else achieve their dreams. Therefore, when you live others, you can help others achieve their dreams.

It is very important to be aware of your behaviors/actions/habits. Habits are significant to be aware of. Habits are something that you do habitually every single day or every week, something that you do repeatedly, that's a habit. However, some people are not aware of their negative habits, which can keep them from achieving their dreams. Therefore, it is very important to be aware of your habits.

If you have a negative habit, then you have the ability once you become aware to actually shift that to a positive habit. Take time now to reflect on some of your negative habits. What can you do to change your negative habits into positive habits?

You can do it. I believe in you. It is just time now for you to believe in yourself.

Fill In the Blank

1. Are you living your dreams?

   _____

2. Are you ready to stop drifting in your life?

   _____

3. Do you believe in yourself?

   _____

Chapter Nineteen

STEP ONTO THE FRONT LINES

Faith over Fear

Faith is believing in the things that you cannot see. Oftentimes, people say, " Well, I understand God's plans for my life," or, "I see the open door, but I am afraid to step into it." It's very important to understand faith over fear, because when you can believe in the things that are not seen, then you are not living in fear, and that means that you are letting go and letting God, and you understand that He is in full control, and when you do that, then you can walk through the door that God has for you. It's right in front of you.

Therefore, you need to have a cleansing moment where you realize that you need to release that fear and the negative energy and keep the faith.

Have you ever had an opportunity right in front of you, but you let it go? My question to you is why did you do that? Most likely, your answer is fear. However, always remember, that fear is the following:

F:Face
E:Everything
A:And
R:Rise

In order to face everything and rise, you need to acknowledge that you may have a fearful state of mind. Therefore, it goes back to awareness. Once you are aware of that behavior, then you can actually find the solution to that behavior, and that solution to that behavior is actually controlling that behavior, because that is an emotional behavior that you have.

Therefore, you need to find balance. This goes back to emotional intelligence; you need to have emotional intelligence and maintain it. Once you maintain your emotional intelligence and you keep it in order, then you can accomplish anything.

Fill In the Blank

1. Are you living in fear?

   _____

2. Are you ready to have faith as small as a mustard seed?

   _____

3. What does emotional intelligence mean to you ?

   _____

Chapter Twenty

YOU ARE ON THE FRONT LINES WITH EACH INDIVIDUAL

Who is God's Servant. Keep Going and Serve!

Be the voice for the voiceless.
You are ready to be on the front lines with each individual who is God's servant. Keep going and serve. The time is now.

Now, as a royal warrior on the front lines, it is very important for you to understand that you need to be the voice for the voiceless. Your voice is a gift from God, but often, a traumatic event may occur in your life that tries to take your voice from you. You may not even realize that your voice is taken from you until years later or until years down the line, but that's why I am here to tell you now that you need to utilize your voice—because it is a beautiful gift.

When you utilize your voice, then you become the voice for the voiceless.

You are someone else's hope. Just by people listening to your voice, alone, it can change their life. You can save someone's life just by sharing your voice.

That's right: your voice is powerful. Do you know how many people are waiting to hear your voice? For example, similar to a doctor, the doctor knows what to do, the doctor has the equipment to save someone's life. Therefore, the doctor has two things to save someone's life: (1) knowledge and (2) equipment. Imagine, if the Doctor did not utilize those two things to save someone's life. Can you imagine that? No, you probably can't, because it is not something that someone should have to think about. Just like this example, you, too, should not think twice about using your voice, if it can save someone's life. It's like having bread and letting someone starve. Would you do that?

Always remember, as a royal warrior on the front lines, your voice is equivalent to the knowledge and equipment of a doctor: you have the ability to save someone's life.

Therefore, it is required that you stay focused on God's purpose for your life on the front lines, serving His people. Never give up and stay focused on the front lines and serving.

Fill In the Blank

1. Are you ready to serve God's people on the next level, royal warrior?

   _____

www.ingramcontent.com/pod-product-compliance
Lightning Source LLC
LaVergne TN
LVHW011855060526
838200LV00054B/4342